My World of Science

SOLIDS, LIQUIDS, AND GASES

Angela Royston

Heinemann Library
Chicago, Illinois

Customer Service 888-454-2279

Visit our website at www.heinemannlibrary.com

Designed by bigtop
Originated by Ambassador Litho
Printed and bound in Hong Kong/China

06 05 04
10 9 8 7 6 5 4

Library of Congress Cataloging-in-Publication Data

Royston, Angela.
  Solids, liquids, and gasses.
       p. cm. -- (My world of science)
Includes bibliographical references and index.
  ISBN 1-58810-245-9 (lib. bdg.)
 1. Matter--Properties--Juvenile literature. 2. Change of state
(Physics)--Juvenile literature. [1. Matter.] I. Title.
  QC173.36 .R69 2001
  530.4--dc21
                                00-012874

Acknowledgments
The author and publishers are grateful to the following for permission to reproduce copyright material:
Trevor Clifford, pp. 6, 7, 8, 9, 12, 14, 15, 16, 17, 18, 19, 20, 21, 22, 23, 26; Eye Ubiquitous, p. 29; Robert Harding, pp. 5, 10, 24; John Marshall/Agstock/Science Photo Library, p. 11; Pictor, p. 28; H. Rogers/Trip, p. 27; Stone, pp. 4, 13, 25.

Cover photograph reproduced with permission of Pictor.

Every effort has been made to contact copyright holders of any material reproduced in this book. Any omissions will be rectified in subsequent printings if notice is given to the publisher.

Some words are shown in bold, like this. You can find out what they mean by looking in the glossary.

Contents

Solids, Liquids, and Gases

Everything in the world is either solid, liquid, or gas. Trees, rocks, and buildings are solid. Rivers and lakes are liquid, and the air is gas.

Solids have a shape you can feel.
Liquids are wet, and take the shape of
their **container.** You usually cannot
see or feel gases, but we know they
are there.

What Is a Solid?

This dinosaur is a solid. A solid is something that has a definite shape. You can feel its shape when you touch it.

Each of these solids has a different shape. What shape is the ball? What shape is the book?

Hard or Soft?

Some solids are hard and some are soft. This dinosaur is made of hard plastic. When you press it, it does not change shape under your fingers.

This teddy bear is soft. When you
press its fur, your fingers make
a **dent.** When you move your fingers,
the dent goes away.

Rough or Smooth?

You can use your fingertips to find out whether something is **smooth** or **rough.** The metal frame of the bicycle is so smooth that it is shiny.

The leaves of this tree are smooth, but the apples are smoother. The bark on the branches of the tree is rough— much rougher than the leaves.

Changing Shape

Some things change shape easily. You can make many different shapes from modeling clay. Try stretching it and pressing it.

Some things can be bent into a different shape. A rope can be twisted and tied into a knot. The branch of a tree can bend too.

Tiny Pieces

Some solids are broken up into tiny pieces. Baby powder, flour, and salt are sold in tiny pieces because they are easier to use like that.

Solids in tiny pieces are often called powders. Flour can be poured from one **container** to another. It can also be poured into a **heap.**

Liquids

Liquids can be poured from one **container** to another too, but they cannot form a **heap.** A liquid always takes the shape of its container.

When you pour juice from a carton into a glass, it becomes a different shape. What happens when the juice spills?

Thick or Thin?

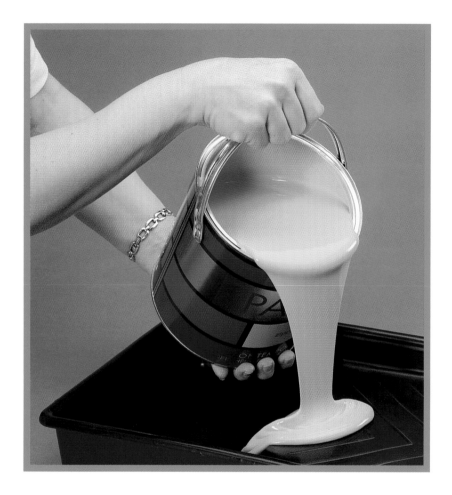

Some liquids are so thick that they can hardly be poured at all. The paint in this can is very thick. It **flows** very slowly.

Thin liquids flow faster than thick ones. Gravy is thinner than yogurt and flows faster than yogurt does. Milk and water flow faster than gravy.

Mixing Solids and Liquids

Some solids and liquids can be mixed together. When you add some powdered paint to water, the water changes color.

When you add salt to water, the salt seems to disappear! In fact, the salt has **dissolved.** You can tell the salt is still there by tasting the water.

Gases

A gas has no particular shape. It floats and spreads out to fill the space it is in. The space in the bottle above the liquid perfume is filled with perfume gas.

You cannot usually see or feel a gas. When you open the bottle of perfume, the gas moves out of the bottle. That is why you can smell the perfume.

Air

You cannot see the air, but it is all around you. You can feel it blowing on a windy day. The air is a mixture of gases.

One of the gases in the air is oxygen.
People, horses, and all living things
breathe in oxygen. We all need
oxygen to stay alive.

Melting and Freezing

When solids are heated, they **melt** and change into liquid. Chocolate is usually solid, but it melts when it is heated and becomes liquid and runny.

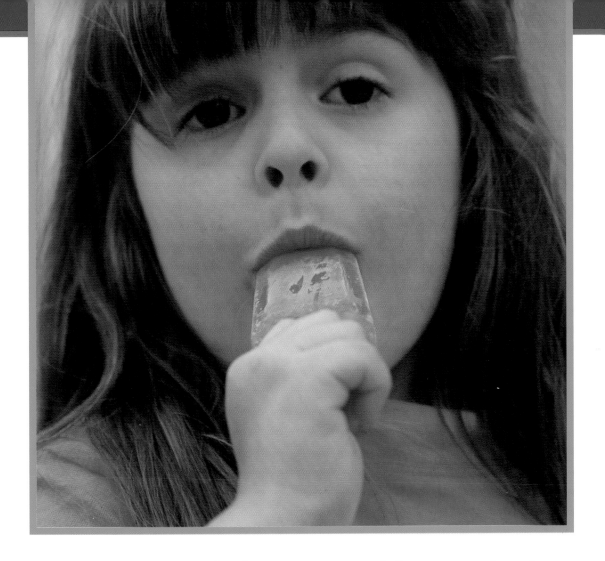

When liquids become cold enough, they **freeze** and change into a solid. This frozen juice bar was made by freezing liquid juice. It melts as it gets warm.

Ice, Water, and Steam

Water usually exists as a liquid, but it can be a solid or a gas too. When water **freezes,** it changes to solid ice. What is happening to these icicles?

When water is heated, it begins to boil.
Bubbles of gas form in the hot water.
The gas floats into the air and forms
very hot steam.

Glossary

breathe to take in and give out air

container something that you can put things in—for example, a box or jar

dent slight mark in a solid

dissolve to mix together and disappear in a liquid

flow to move smoothly

freeze when a liquid gets very cold and becomes solid

heap pile

melt when a solid gets warmer and becomes a liquid

rough bumpy or uneven

smooth having an even surface

More Books to Read

Glover, David. *Solids and Liquids.* New York: Larousse Kingfisher Chambers, Inc., 1995. An older reader can help you with this book.

Hewitt, Sally. *Solid, Liquid, or Gas?* Danbury, Conn.: Children's Press, 1998.

Robinson, Fay. *Solid, Liquid, Gas!* Danbury, Conn.: Children's Press, 1996.

Index